Faith Footprints with My Grandchild

BroadStreet

P U B L I S H I N G

BroadStreet Publishing Group, LLC
Racine, Wisconsin, USA
BroadStreetPublishing.com

Faith Footprints with My Grandchild

By Dr. Mary Manz Simon
Copyright © 2016 Mary Manz Simon LLC

Published in association with the literary agency, WTA Services LLC, Franklin, TN

ISBN-13: 978-1-4245-5213-9 (hardcover)
ISBN-13: 978-1-4245-5214-6 (e-book)

Cover design by Chris Garborg at GarborgDesign.com
Typesetting by Kjell Garborg at GarborgDesign.com

Printed in China
16 17 18 19 20   5 4 3 2 1

Contents

Introduction

A grandchild is an amazing bonus blessing who allows us to practice true lifestyle Christianity. Maximizing moments with these precious children allows us to leave footprints of faith for another generation.

What a privilege that we never need to question whether or not we still have a purpose for living! For during these years when we appear to lose so much—our health, our eyebrows, even our pets—God gifts us with a child. As a result, each new day overflows with possibilities.

This time around, we are not new moms, perched on the edge of a sometimes frightening path into the unknown. Now, we are life veterans. We bring wisdom, experience, and a clear sense of what is important. We know that the age at which a child is toilet-trained or learns to ride a bike doesn't really matter. And so we listen as a child describes baby birdies in the nest. We attempt to understand a complex science project and communicate with a child who breathes digital. The gift of time to a grandchild becomes a gift we give ourselves.

Topics in this volume highlight issues related to nurturing the faith of the next generation. Each of the fifty-two entries begins with words of encouragement and inspiration. Grandmother-specific prayer themes and activities are followed by space to record and date your reflections, ideas, or plans.

You may have already discovered that being a grandmother also ushers in a new stage of our personal faith walk as truths from years past take on a deeper meaning. Today, my love for God and family overflows across the miles and years. Even during the autumn of life, I sing a new song with the psalmist and shout, "Praise the Lord. I'm a grandma!"

Mary Manz Simon

1

My Smiling Heart

Shout for joy to the Lord, everyone on earth.
Burst into joyful songs and make music.
PSALM 98:4 NIRV

"Say cheese."

How many times have you said that? Because a perfect picture of a grandchild is worth the effort, we dance with a monkey on our head or wiggle our ears while singing nonsense syllables. The results of our efforts can capture a priceless image of that moment in time.

Merely anticipating a visit from a grandchild puts a smile on our face. As children of God, we can journey through each day with a smiling heart, but having a grandchild gives us another source of delight. Knowing that God loves us and that precious child fills us with the same boundless joy recorded by the psalmist.

Even a very young grandchild can "shout," "burst into joyful songs," and "make music," to use the words of the psalmist. Those are all natural expressions of sheer delight. But typically, those instinctive responses to God's goodness become less obvious and less frequent as we get older.

Yet, regardless of our age, we can reflect childlike glee simply knowing that God's love overflows from the inside out. Looking for the little things that we take for granted in life, as well the immense blessings of being a grandmother, entitles us to begin today and every day with a smiling heart.

To Do with My Grandchild

Share your smiling heart. Charities that are swamped with volunteers before Christmas frequently echo with deafening silence after the holiday; call ahead to see when your help would be most beneficial. Also check with your church office for the names of shut-in members of the church or community who would welcome a visit from you and your grandchild. Take along family photos from the holidays to use as conversation starters.

To Pray

Dear God,

My heart overflows with the joy of knowing you. Now that I have a grandchild who also shares that love, I want to "shout" and "burst into joyful songs" like the psalmist. May I begin and end each day with a smiling heart that reflects your bounteous love. Amen.

To Reflect

My grandchild sees a reflection of my smiling heart when...

_____

_____

_____

_____

_____

_____

_____

_____

_____

_____

_____

_____

_____

_____

_____

_____

_____

2
Let's Talk

LORD, every morning you hear my voice.
Every morning, I tell you what I need,
and I wait for your answer.

PSALM 5:3

"Do you want to talk with Grandma?"

"No," replied the boys, one after another. Even the lure of talking on a new phone didn't entice a single child.

How ironic that when we finally set aside time to talk with the children in our lives, they are often too busy to do so. Basketball, afterschool activities, and even preschool playgroups have a higher priority than chatting with a gray-haired lady. I'm grateful that on another day those same children will engage in a lengthy conversation with me.

When life interferes with real-time talk, I'm reminded that someone always has an ear to listen. God is busy with the entire world, but He's never too busy to hear from a grandma. Prayer is such a blessing. How often I appreciate this 24/7-anytime-anywhere availability. There are no pause buttons or service interruptions. God always listens not only to the words I say, but the heart-speak I don't dare whisper.

I count on prayer. I depend on God being there for me. I am confident that God will hear not only my words, but also the prayers I offer on behalf of the children who are too busy playing video games and shooting hoops to talk to Him today.

To Do with My Grandchild

Pray your way through the beginning of the New Year. Gather all the holiday cards or greetings you received. Or work your way, line by line, through your e-mail address book. Remember one person each day. On days when you pray for someone that both you and your grandchild know, phone or text your grandchild so you can pray together. Children are often amazed at how frequently grandmothers have conversations with God.

To Pray

Thank you, God, for your listening ear. Remind my grandchild to call on you throughout life. Bless those little talks with you, so that he learns what I know—that you will always listen. Amen.

To Reflect

As I remember my childhood prayers, I want my grandchild to...

_____

_____

_____

_____

_____

_____

_____

_____

_____

_____

_____

_____

_____

_____

_____

3

Maximize the Moments

Make the most of every opportunity.

EPHESIANS 5:16 NIRV

The arrival of a grandchild signals the beginning of a new season of life. The effort of chasing after a toddler or climbing down from the top bleacher of a school gym offers a vivid reminder that being a grandmother means we are growing older. Though we belong to the healthiest generation of grandparents in history, aging catches up with even the most fit and agile.

Instead of focusing on what we can't do, we can use how we cope with the aging process as a teachable moment for a grandchild. Even a preschooler, who has not yet learned to read words, reads emotions. That child observes how we approach the day. She sees and hears how we react when an unexpected problem pops up, and notices if we go to the gym or if the pages move in our Bible.

In countless ways, we echo the words of St. Paul to the people of Ephesus—to "make the most of every opportunity." If you put your grandchild to bed, do you have an extra five minutes before lights-out? Tell your grandchild who first talked to you about Jesus. Are you waiting in awkward silence for someone to offer a mealtime prayer? Take the lead. Do you want to help but can't shovel snow anymore? Have hot chocolate waiting in the kitchen. Showing a grandchild how to make the most of every opportunity is a biblical lesson that will last a lifetime.

To Do with My Grandchild

Keep a "things to do with my grandchild" list. Even if your next visit is far in the future, looking ahead will keep you focused forward, anticipating your time together. Ask your grandchild to keep a list too. When a significant amount of time passes between visits, a child can outgrow proposed activities. Looking at his list will give you insight into his developmental level.

To Pray

Dear God,
Thank you for giving me time with my grandchild. Lead us in ways to experience your love in the time we spend together. Help me memorize the moments so I can hold them in my heart. Amen.

To Reflect

The first time I thought seriously about being a grandmother...

_____

_____

_____

_____

_____

_____

_____

_____

_____

_____

_____

_____

_____

_____

_____

4

More than Fun

Clap your hands, all you people. Shout to God with joy.

PSALM 47:1

Are you having fun?

One challenge of growing older is that we don't always experience fun with the same degree of exuberance that we did in the past. Some might say, "That's why God gave us a grandchild." Those observers might be correct.

A grandchild nudges us to attempt, sample, and participate in ways we probably wouldn't try on our own. It's fun making snowballs or cheering on a basketball team, but as Christian grandmothers, we can savor more than merely good times. We can have joy.

The word "joy" is used more than one hundred and fifty times in the Bible. That number is probably not surprising, because joy begins by journeying with Jesus. Quite simply, when we walk with God, we experience joy. This is a fruit of the spirit, or a reward for walking in faith (Galatians 5:22).

Joy doesn't just add sparkle to happy days; it prevents sadness from deepening. That's meaningful, because walking in faith doesn't protect us from difficulties and problems. However, even when life bounces us around, having an inner core of joy lifts us up. Regardless of what happens, we are assured of God's love. When we tell our grandchild, "I love you and God loves you," we communicate keys to a joy-filled life.

To Do with My Grandchild

Make a skinny snowman. Use a fine-point marker to draw a face and buttons on an individually wrapped piece of string cheese. Add a ribbon for a scarf. Glue a wrapped chocolate kiss on the top for a silvery hat. Extend the fun by experiencing joy when you and your grandchild give away the snowmen.

To Pray

Dear God,
Your goodness makes my heart bubble over with joy. Help me draw on that joy when times are tough. Lead me to share this joy with others, especially my grandchild.

To Reflect

When we are together, my grandchild experiences joy...

_____

_____

_____

_____

_____

_____

_____

_____

_____

_____

_____

_____

_____

_____

_____

_____

_____

_____

5

Smart and Smarter

Everyone with good sense wants to learn.
PROVERBS 18:15 CEV

A young grandchild is so smart. He knows it doesn't matter if the roof leaks; after all, it's fun to catch drops in a bucket. She won't mind having a snack on a chipped plate; she still gets to lick the frosting off a cupcake. Those little kids are very bright.

As grandchildren grow up, they begin to notice things like a cracked front step and the fence that needs painting. But they don't mind, because they're even smarter now. After years of spending time with us, they have learned that our homes and our hearts overflow with God's love and our love.

What a blessing that grandchildren have a perspective that is blind to the unimportant. When we're together, they often zero in on what matters. If we had this type of love, we would see beyond the petty irritating issues that can consume so much emotional energy.

We often think of teaching grandchildren how to *do* things. Perhaps, though, we could be learning from them how to *see* things. After all, focusing on the big stuff would simplify life. Plus, if we ignored the little things, we'd be happier.

In addition to having a *loving* relationship with our grandchildren, we can have a *learning* relationship. We can not only be the teacher, but also the student. Have you ever wondered, *What can I learn next time a grandchild visits?*

To Do with My Grandchild

Play school. Show your grandchild how to do something, and then let your grandchild be the teacher. God created us to move, so doing this outside (even in the snow!) offers multiple possibilities for large-muscle activities and sports. Be prepared for lots of laughs. Thank God for the various muscles, tendons, ligaments, and joints that allow you the strength and flexibility to move.

To Pray

Dear God,
Prepare my heart for learning. Tear down any attitudes that keep me from being "teachable." As I continue to grow, help me take advantage of opportunities that will give both my grandchild and me greater understanding of you, each other, and the world you've created. Amen.

To Reflect

When I think about my grandchild teaching me something, I...

_____

_____

_____

_____

_____

_____

_____

_____

_____

_____

_____

_____

_____

_____

_____

_____

6

From Darkness to Light

I thought about all my hard work, and I felt depressed.

ECCLESIASTES 2:20 CEV

Scholars are uncertain who wrote Ecclesiastes. Many attribute the book to the wise and wealthy King Solomon; other experts disagree. Although today's verse is a dark passage, countless grandmothers identify with its sentiment.

Perhaps you're among those women who faithfully took children to Sunday school, taught them about Jesus, and said bedtime prayers. Now adults, some of those children have moved away from church, and even away from God. Our hearts are broken as grandchildren grow up without knowing Jesus as their Savior. It's not surprising that some of us echo the words of the biblical writer: "I thought about all my hard work, and I felt depressed."

But God doesn't leave us in that dark place. Our Savior offers words of comfort that only He can give. When Jesus stood on Solomon's Porch in the temple in Jerusalem, He said, "My sheep listen to my voice. I know them, and they follow me" (John 10:27 NIrV).

Jesus hasn't forgotten our children or our grandchildren. God knows the needs of our loved ones; He hears our prayers. The Good Shepherd will continue to search for the sheep who have wandered away, so they can join us in celebrating the joy salvation brings (Matthew 18:12). His heart, like ours, spills over with love for the wayward sheep. His arms, like ours, are open, waiting to welcome them.

To Do with My Grandchild

Ask friends to share their experiences with the power of prayer. While you faithfully remember your loved ones in prayer, learn about others who have prayed faithfully.

Be encouraged by the story of Monica, which has been retold for centuries. Through an arranged marriage, this Christian woman became the wife of a drunk who was violent and unfaithful. One of their children lived a wild life, used alcohol and drugs, and became involved with a cult. But day after day, year after year, Monica prayed that both her husband and son would accept Christ. Before his death, her husband became a Christian. Monica continued to pray for her son. Those prayers were finally answered, for we know Monica's son as St. Augustine, one of the great leaders of the early church.

To Pray

Dear God,
Thank you for people who encourage me and my family. Hear my prayer for those whom I love so deeply. May I fall asleep tonight remembering the Good Shepherd who continues to search for the wandering sheep. Amen.

To Reflect

As I pray for those whom I love, I am confident that God...

_____

_____

_____

_____

_____

_____

_____

_____

_____

_____

_____

_____

_____

_____

_____

_____

_____

7

The Lineage of God's Love

But you remain the same, and your years will never end.

PSALM 102:27 NIV

The word "connection" might trigger thoughts of Skyping last night or responding to a grandchild's text this morning. But as grandmothers, we are connected in an even more significant way, both to the past and to the future.

The women who came before us helped shape the women we are today. Being next in a family lineage gives us more than genetic DNA. Corresponding with an aunt, talking with a great-grandmother, or having a heart-to-heart with our own mother allows us to tap into her life experiences. Even if we aren't best buddies, our woman-to-woman dialogue can reach an intimate level almost immediately.

As a grandmother, we are also uniquely linked to the next generation. We draw on the past to help a grandchild focus forward. The issues a grandchild faces—online privacy, pop culture influences, bullying—have a contemporary veneer, but the experiences and solutions have an underlying familiarity to those of the past.

God has a "sameness" that is comforting. The God my mother worshipped, and I prayed to as a child, is the same God who watches over my grandchildren. There's a value in that consistency through the years. God watched over the women who came before me. He has led me to this moment. He will be there for my grandchild. His seamless, constant love is a blessing through the years.

To Do with My Grandchild

Find a picture of your grandchild at a younger age. With your grandchild, compare it to a recent photo or a picture you take today. Repeat the comparisons using images of other family members including yourself. As you examine the "then" and "now" photos, talk about how God never, ever changes. This will demonstrate for your grandchild, in a very personal way, the unchanging nature of God.

To Pray

Dear God,
Knowing that you haven't changed and won't ever change has given me such comfort through the years. As I've transitioned from being a mom to being a grandmother, the transformation has been somewhat startling at times. Assurance that you will "remain the same" for me, my grandchild, and future generations gives me a sense of peace. Amen.

To Reflect

One thing that I hope never changes about my grandchild is...

_____

_____

_____

_____

_____

_____

_____

_____

_____

_____

_____

_____

_____

_____

_____

8

Sibling Rivalry

None of you should look out just for your own good.
Each of you should also look out for the good of others.

PHILIPPIANS 2:4 NIrV

The equation is simple: two children + one grandmother = sibling rivalry.

Grandchildren will always crave your time and attention, your lap and your love. Although it's wonderful to be cherished so deeply, sharing yourself this way can cause problems for everyone.

Years ago, we coped with sibling rivalry among our children; now, even though it doesn't seem fair, we need to face this issue again. Of course, sibling rivalry has been a problem since the days of Cain and Abel. When God accepted Abel's offering, Cain got so angry that he murdered his brother. We read in the Bible that sibling rivalry is a natural reflection of our sinful human nature, so it's here to stay (Psalm 51:5).

From a child's perspective, the amount of time you spend is seen as a measure of your love, so set aside time for each grandchild. Unless you plan to use a screen together during the designated time, turn of all technology.

A natural parallel is the time we spend with God. Unless we're doing devotions on the phone or reading Scripture on a tablet, our time with Him is free of distractions and interruptions. You'll make an indelible impression by saying to your grandchild, "I turn off everything when I talk to God, and I turn off everything when I talk with you."

To Do with My Grandchild

We naturally see each grandchild as the unique person God created, without the labels siblings might attach or the expectations parents set. The next time you are with your grandchild, find ways to celebrate that specialness. Take a budding artist to an art exhibit. Play duets (even if one-handed) with a grandchild who is taking piano lessons. Bundle up and search for signs of spring with a young child whose personality is just emerging. Concentrate with a laser-like focus to celebrate the individuality of the grandchild God created in His image.

To Pray

Dear God,
I am grateful for each grandchild. Help me draw attention to the special skills and abilities that make each one unique. May each child identify, utilize, and thank you for their special gifts. Amen.

To Reflect

Focusing on each child as an individual helps...

_____

_____

_____

_____

_____

_____

_____

_____

_____

_____

_____

_____

_____

_____

_____

_____

_____

_____

_____

9

Be a God-Link

We will tell the next generation the praiseworthy deeds of the LORD,
his power, and the wonders he has done.

PSALM 78:4 NIV

I'm not the only one sitting in an empty pew. Even after years of taking children to church and today's high-tech packaging with lights-camera-action, many grandchildren do not regularly participate in worship. For many, Sunday has become a "family day" for doing things together. While that's admirable, "God's family day" has been re-defined. As a result, many grandmas sit alone in church. However, each of us can still be a meaningful God-link for our grandchildren.

Whether or not children are regular church-goers, kids of all ages ask questions about death, God, and the afterlife. To become a God-link in a grandchild's life, we grab every opportunity to not only answer questions and discuss faith-related issues, but to also offer resources.

Some grandmothers take grandchildren to a bookstore for their birthday and allow them to choose a new Bible for the year. As time passes, each child develops a sizeable Christian library from simple Bible storybooks to hefty study Bibles. A gift card to an online Christian bookstore is especially convenient for long-distance celebrations. Gifting a child with Christian jewelry or apparel provides other options.

We might attend church without a grandchild, but God can still use us in numerous and even unexpected ways to help a grandchild grow up with Jesus.

To Do with My Grandchild

Today, identify at least one news story with the potential to begin a conversation about faith-related issues with your grandchild. You might read an online sports story, watch a TV feature about house renovation, or read a magazine article. The current Information Age overflows with content related to morals, ethical behavior, and faith. The photo of a football hero or a funny video is sure to generate at least a glance from an older child. For a younger child, snap a quick photo of something outdoors that reminds you of the Creator or take a selfie while reading your Bible or this devotional. If your grandchild is online, forward the image or video clip with a note. Snail-mailing works too, because all children enjoy opening mail addressed to them. After you begin this list of talking points, continually update the options.

To Pray

Dear God,

Help me capitalize on opportunities to talk about faith-related issues with my grandchild. Give me the right words to say and the confidence to go through the doors you open. Equip me, Lord, to be an effective God-link for my grandchild. Amen.

To Do with My Grandchild

A legacy is what we leave behind. It can include models of behavior, money or other possessions, and gifts of service, time, or talents. Identify the legacy you received from family members, mentors, and friends. How are those legacies influencing what you will leave your grandchildren?

To Pray

Dear God,
Help me to appreciate the past as I look forward to the future. May the legacy I leave make a difference in the lives of those I leave behind, especially my grandchildren. Amen.

To Reflect

A legacy worth leaving my grandchildren is...

_____

_____

_____

_____

_____

_____

_____

_____

_____

_____

_____

_____

_____

_____

_____

_____

11

Listen Up

He says, "Be still, and know that I am God."

PSALM 46:10 NIrV

A grandchild gives us many things—a picture for the refrigerator, a purpose for living, a tight hug. But a grandchild can also teach us to listen.

"Do you hear that?" Our grandchild shushes us, pointing to the bird warbling a cheery song.

"Do you hear that?" Our grandchild watches a garbage truck lumber past, staring until the vehicle is completely out of sight.

"Do you hear that?" we might ask, catching on to the game. Because grandchildren see life through a different lens and move at a different pace, they notice things that we miss. We simply can't pay attention to everything; in today's fast-paced world, we would end up like a spinning top. But in our hurry to move forward, we sometimes miss something important.

The Old Testament prophet Elijah was guilty of that. Running from a wicked queen, he sought refuge in a cave. Elijah listened for God in a whooshing wind, rumbling earthquake, and hissing fire. The prophet finally heard God in a whisper.

We are busy women. The noise of life can be deafening. But when we hit pause, we might hear a plea for advice from our adult child, buried under meaningless chatter. Hidden beneath outrageous behavior, we might hear a grandchild seeking affirmation.

God says, "Be still, and know that I am God." When we stop running, we find the peace that faith offers.

To Do with My Grandchild

"Read it again!" (And again and again.) Do you groan when your grandchild repeatedly asks you to read the same book? A child feels secure hearing a favorite story; after all, he knows exactly what happens. That's comforting in a world that changes as quickly as ours. A grandchild who listens to familiar Bible stories read from various books and versions of the Bible, has an even more important take away: Although the words might vary from one book to another, the lessons from the Bible will always be the same.

To Pray

Dear God,
It's awesome that you want to communicate with me. Slow me down when I find it hard to stop and listen for your voice. Amen.

To Reflect

Knowing that my grandchild hears the same words from the Bible that I heard as a child, reminds me...

_____

_____

_____

_____

_____

_____

_____

_____

_____

_____

_____

_____

_____

_____

_____

_____

The Ripple Effect

Each generation will announce to the next your
wonderful and powerful deeds.

PSALM 145:4 CEV

We have been blessed. Science and medicine have given us the prospect of a life longer than the biblical fourscore years and ten. Simply stated, we have the potential to spend more time with grandchildren than grandmothers in any previous generation.

Technology and computer science have provided more new ways to share our stories. No other generation of grandmothers has had the wealth and variety of tools, online and offline, to record and share our life stories.

These innovations expand the effect we can have, all because of what happens through one of God's creations, the ripple effect. When a pebble is dropped in a pond, ripples extend in circles beyond the point where the pebble plopped. When we share our life story, it goes to our children, our grandchildren, and on to future generations.

But there's more, because the ways that the Holy Spirit has worked through the years is woven throughout our personal storyline. Grandchildren and others become aware of God's actions as reflected in one simple life—ours. Like Jacob in the Old Testament, we might not have even been aware of the many times God was at work in our lives (Genesis 28:16). But like ripples in the pond, the story of God with Jacob and now God in our life continues to be shared through the years.

To Do with My Grandchild

Looking back through a prayer journal, personal diary, or family photo album can reveal times when God was at work in our lives. As you replay family videos and page through heirloom albums with grandchildren, take the opportunity to point out ways that God was at work: the auto accident in which you weren't hurt, the wonderful weather for a wedding, the doctor who delivered your own child in the middle of the night. Your grandchild will begin to understand how God continues writing all our life stories.

To Pray

Dear God,
Looking back, I see so many times when you have led me, protected me, or been a presence in my life. Looking ahead, continue to be with me and my family members who are so precious, especially my grandchildren. Amen.

To Reflect

When I feel God's hand on my shoulder...

_____

_____

_____

_____

_____

_____

_____

_____

_____

_____

_____

_____

_____

_____

_____

_____

_____

13

Company's Coming

Be sure to welcome strangers into your home. By doing this,
some people have welcomed angels as guests, without even knowing it.

HEBREWS 13:2 CEV

After years of hosting play groups, birthday parties, and family gatherings, we've certainly gained experience caring for guests. Even if hospitality is not our spiritual gift, being a gracious host eventually becomes easier with practice. We continue to have multiple opportunities to be hospitable.

Have you ever welcomed an angel? The writer of the Hebrews says, "Be sure to welcome strangers into your home. By doing this, some people have welcomed angels as guests, without even knowing it."

After all, that's what happened to Abraham. One day, three travelers appeared at his tent door. Abraham was considerate to these unexpected guests, leading them to a shady place under a tree. He was an accommodating host, offering water to wash their dusty feet. He served them fresh food and poured them drinks. Abraham was so gracious that his guests had the opportunity to "refresh their hearts" (Genesis 18:5 NKJV). That hospitality was a natural expression of his love for God.

During these grandmothering years, our family circle continues to expand and change shape. We might meet a grandchild's esteemed coach or welcome a new step-grandchild. Hosting people who are new to us implies we have opportunities to not only model Christ-like caring, but also, like Abraham, perhaps even welcome an angel.

To Do with My Grandchild

In previous generations, practicing good manners and knowing how to act in social situations was built into everyday activities. But times have changed. Does your grandchild know how to make a guest feel welcome? Set aside time to practice basic etiquette. To increase the fun factor, persuade a grandfather, child's sibling, or even the family dog to serve as the guest. Then ask your grandchild to practice seating a guest, introducing you to a guest, and initiating polite conversation. Conclude by letting your grandchild serve the cookies the two of you baked together. Encourage her in the words of Scripture to "use your best manners" (Proverbs 23:1b CEV).

To Pray

Dear God,

Let the love I feel for you be reflected in how both my grandchild and I treat others. Guide my actions and attitude so that I am hospitable and accommodating. Enlighten me to show that same consideration and respect for others when I am far from home. Amen.

To Reflect

One way I can help my grandchild develop a heart that is hospitable is...

_____

_____

_____

_____

_____

_____

_____

_____

_____

_____

_____

_____

_____

_____

_____

_____

14

You're Valuable

His lord said to him, "Well done, good and faithful servant."
MATTHEW 25:21 NKJV

How much is a mother worth?

As the demands on moms appear to multiply (and technology was supposed to make life easier, remember?), media outlets annually sum up the monetary value of a mom. That amount rises each year.

However, I've never heard a total that estimates the worth of grandmothers. Consider what we offer. Endless hugs. Unconditional love. Christian values. A lifetime of experience with children. And that's merely for starters.

Perhaps, even though you are called a "Grand Granny" or "Irreplaceable Mimi," you also feel a bit undervalued. That's understandable. The effort we put forth takes more out of us as we get older. Although we affirm others, sometimes others forget to acknowledge us, as if gray hair makes us fade into the background. Our behind-the-scenes serving doesn't always generate a "Thank you."

Long ago, Mary, the mother of James the Less and Joses, served in the background. She and other women (perhaps some grandmothers) supported Jesus and His disciples. On Good Friday, Mary even stayed at the cross. Then she and the other women collected burial spices and went to the tomb.

On Easter morning, Mary was rewarded for her faithfulness. The angel announced the resurrection to her and the women who had been in the background. These women brought the news of the resurrection to the disciples.

In whatever way we give to others, God recognizes our service, saying, "Well done, good and faithful servant."

To Do with My Grandchild

Play "hidden helper" with your grandchild. Spend an entire day keeping track of how you help others. Don't let other family members know you are doing this. At the end of the day, count how often the two of you were hidden helpers.

When you share your secret serving with family members, everyone might want to join in the game. An understanding of compassionate serving in the early years can lay the foundation for developing empathy, as a grandchild begins to feel satisfaction by helping others.

To Pray

Dear God,
Thank you for the examples of such faithful women in the Bible. Help me to look for ways I can reach out to serve. Help my grandchild to grow up knowing the joy of serving others. Amen.

To Reflect

When I see my grandchild serving others gladly...

_____

_____

_____

_____

_____

_____

_____

_____

_____

_____

_____

_____

_____

_____

_____

_____

_____

15
Real-Time Reflections

What happens now has happened in the past,
and what will happen in the future has happened before.

ECCLESIASTES 3:15

Once wasn't enough.

Once again, we suffer through "Twinkle, Twinkle, Little Star" played on a squeaky violin. Once again, we shiver on the sidelines while players chase a ball up a muddy field. And we buy a child a cookie after a successful shopping trip (because bribery still works.)

This is all part of nurturing a second (or third) generation. Holidays create Hallmark moments for family memory books and videos, but everyday activities provide the basic fabric of a grandmother's life.

Reflections of real-time faith are also woven into daily life. When you're running errands, does your grandchild listen for a siren? Perhaps you've taught your grandchild to pray for first responders, just as you taught your own child years ago. Or perhaps your grandchild automatically reaches for your hand to form a mealtime prayer circle. That was a ritual when you were raising your child too, whether you were eating in a fast food restaurant or in the kitchen at home.

These actions don't include memorized church-talk; instead, they're real-time reflections of faith that connect across the generations.

In the New Testament, Jesus taught lessons by using whatever was convenient—the birds flying overhead or the flowers in the field. Once again, we can follow His example, for God continues to move through everyday happenings and situations that unfold in front of us.

To Do with My Grandchild

Every family is shaped by actions or expressions that make them distinctive. In your family, does everyone read before going to bed? Does everyone carry a Bible to church? Do children hold hands when crossing a parking lot? Identify everyday rituals and traditions that define your family, then the next time you talk with other grandmothers, ask about their family distinctions. Listen for ideas worth considering adopting in your own family.

To Pray

Dear God,
Keep me alert for opportunities to weave reflections of faith into everyday activities with my grandchild. Bless those moments when we connect with you. Amen.

To Reflect

One distinction that defines our family is...

16

Neighborliness

"Love your neighbor as you love yourself."

MARK 12:31

As we push a stroller or jog alongside a bike with training wheels, our grandchild's neighborhood can become as familiar as our own. A baby learns to recognize things around him before venturing beyond his neighborhood and community. People who live in the surrounding homes and walk the same streets will eventually become part of our grandchild's comfort zone.

During Bible times, the opportunity to connect with neighbors was almost part of the house design. Some people could simply hop from one flat roof to another. But the current popularity of indoor–outdoor living space has not been accompanied by an automatic increase in neighborliness. This is why community policing efforts stress that the first step toward a safe community is learning the names of those who live nearby.

Children are born with an innate urge to socialize. They don't need to join a "neighborhood watch" to practice the compassionate caring for others that Jesus highlighted in the parable of the Good Samaritan (Luke 10: 25–37). While telling that story, Jesus expanded the meaning of the term "neighbor" to include anyone we meet. Later, St. Paul encouraged the early Christians in Galatia to "love your neighbors as yourself" (Galatian 5:14). Expressing Christian concern for others was a consistent theme in Paul's ministry.

Although we don't scramble across rooftops to visit our next-door neighbor, everyday activities offer numerous opportunities for a grandchild to befriend others. Experiencing neighborliness, while safely under your protection, is an ideal way for a child to put into action the words of St. Paul.

To Do with My Grandchild

Take a neighborhood prayer walk with your grandchild. Simply pause in front of each house to pray for the resident by name. Your grandchild might suggest specific needs or issues to bring to God. Permit your grandchild to respond if someone asks what you are doing; this is a good opportunity to attach words to her Christian actions. If desired, you can both wear disposable gloves and carry a trash bag to collect litter or stray items.

To Pray

Dear God,
May my grandchild experience friendliness in this community. Guide both young and old to appreciate the safety, courtesy, and kindness that results when neighbors care for each other. Amen.

To Reflect

When I think of my grandchild growing up in this place, I...

17

God's Promise for the Future

"For I know the plans I have for you," declares the Lord, "plans to prosper you and not to harm you, plans to give you hope and a future."

JEREMIAH 29:11 NIV

We're quite a group, aren't we?

Although people describe us as the healthiest, wealthiest, and best-educated grandmothers in history, we don't share many common traits. Some grandmothers are barely entering middle age; others don't have a grandchild until late in life. Our incomes vary widely. Thanks to current geographic and social mobility, we have a huge range of experiences and cultural traits. Marketers would be challenged to craft a strategy to reach all of us, unless they targeted the warm spot in each of our hearts that is labeled "grandchild."

Although we are not a homogeneous bunch, each of our lives changed when we became a grandmother. A new person entered our family circle, someone whose likes, dislikes, idiosyncrasies, and personality we needed to learn. We immediately added more photos to the phone and had another birth date to remember. But more importantly, becoming a grandmother gave us another reason to have hope for the future. And isn't that the common denominator? Our grandchild, perhaps still a newborn, reminds us that God has planned a future filled with hope.

We can look past international conflicts and national problems; we can forget our own aches and age spots. Without saying a word, a grandchild reminds us that God intends to give us hope and a future.

To Do with My Grandchild

Numerous people will ask your grandchild, "What do you want to be when you grow up?" Resist the urge to repeat the question. Instead, talk about the various jobs and roles you have had through the years. How did you learn the skills you needed? What problems did you solve? In what ways did God help you? You learned from experiences as you lived them, and your grandchild can learn from your living history.

To Pray

Dear God,
I don't know what the future holds for me or my grandchild, but I am grateful you will guide each of us forward. Equip us to deal with unexpected issues and situations. Help us follow the path you have laid out for us. Amen.

To Reflect

When I think about my grandchild's future, I...

Help for the Brokenhearted

The Lord is close to the brokenhearted
and saves those who are crushed in spirit.

PSALM 34:18 NIV

Although the role of grandmother usually fills our heart with joy, we live in a sinful world and also might suffer from a shattered heart. Even a strong faith doesn't protect us from what happens when relationships are broken. Some grandmothers experience the agony of being kept away from a grandchild; others experience the grief of watching from a distance as a family falls apart. Even the most loving grandmother can have a broken heart.

As women, we prioritize relationships. That's why our initial response might be to dive head first into the situation. We want to fix what's wrong. However, because family matters tend to be complex, solutions might be equally complicated and the timeline for repair and restoration might be lengthy. Instead of being helpful, our well-intentioned actions might be hurtful.

Prayer is the single action that will always help. After all, we know that "if we ask anything according to His will, He hears us. And if we know that He hears us, whatever we ask, we know that we have the petitions that we have asked of Him" (1 John 5:14–15 NKJV). We don't merely talk to God. We pray with complete confidence that He hears us.

This doesn't mean we always get what we want or hope for, but that God promises to heal our broken heart and bandage our wounds (Psalm 147:3).

To Do with My Grandchild

A prayer journal can help us maintain a healthy perspective on the ups and downs of life. Simply take an empty notebook and record the date and your prayers. Leave space to record the way God responded. This simple format works especially well if you and your grandchild both decide to keep journals and then share with each other the key points in your conversations with God. If you purchase a formal prayer journal for your grandchild, purchase a nice one for yourself too. Having an accountability partner adds an element of commitment for both of you.

To Pray

Dear God,
Sometimes my pain is so deep that my heart feels shattered. On days when I struggle and am barely able to cope, lift me up, Lord God. Help those whom I love. Amen.

To Reflect

At times when I need God the most...

_____

_____

_____

_____

_____

_____

_____

_____

_____

_____

_____

_____

_____

_____

_____

_____

_____

19

Love across Generations

It is truly wonderful when relatives live together in peace.
PSALM 133:1 CEV

Intergenerational relationships among women can be so challenging. Expectations, boundaries, and loyalties sometimes cast shadows that extend far beyond generations. Friction can fester across the years. Perhaps that's why the genuine friendship of the biblical widows Naomi and her daughter-in-law, Ruth, is such an uplifting story (Ruth 1:1–18).

Ruth and Naomi might have been at distinctly different points on the timeline of grief. Perhaps they coped with their sadness and loss in contrasting ways. Ruth was a Moabite and Naomi was a Hebrew woman, so even their cultural traditions were dissimilar. And yet, these women formed a deep bond.

Their biblical model can be helpful to us as diversity begins to characterize families today. Although we often assume an older woman will teach the younger one, Ruth and Naomi were willing to learn from each other. Their relationship mirrored commitment and loyalty, but both women were willing to give and take. What a healthy reflection of cross-generational love!

We share the love of our grandchild with at least one other woman, our daughter-in-law. Although comedians use that relationship to generate laughs, the story of Naomi and Ruth emphasizes a healthy cross-generational friendship. Reflecting on their story offers fresh insight to apply to our situation.

To Do with My Grandchild

Make a family tree with your grandchild. Although young children are still trying to understand how people in a family fit together across the years, even they will be intrigued by glimpses of personal history. Share photos of your own children when they were the same age as your grandchild and pictures showing Christian milestones. A grandchild will be especially intrigued by pictures that show her wearing the same baptismal gown as her mom.

To Pray

Dear God,
You have chosen me to be a grandmother in this family. May my relationships grow to reflect the depth of love and loyalty modeled by these women of the Bible so long ago. Amen.

To Reflect

Thinking about my daughter-in-law, I...

20

Grandparenting 101

There are different ways to serve. But they all come from the same Lord.

1 CORINTHIANS 12:5 NIrV

We knew how to mother, or at least we did our best. But do we know how to grandmother?

If you've failed at baby burrito swaddling or thought the indicator strip on the diaper was merely a decoration, perhaps you're ready to register for a grandparent class. We're not alone in the need for knowledge. Actually, so much has changed since we became moms that hospitals and agencies across the country now offer refresher courses for grandparents.

Being a grandma can be so humbling that we might wonder, *Do I have anything worthwhile to share with my grandchild?* But be encouraged. What we do with a grandchild might make an impact, but who we are can make a difference.

Just as God created this precious child with gifts and talents, He created us, too, with gifts and talents. Through the years, we've had time to develop those attributes into a full range of abilities; now a grandchild can see how God has blessed us both.

Talk about what character means when you go to a patriotic event. Show your grandchild where to hang a bag on a wheelchair handle. Connect your commitment to God with how you serve at the church picnic. Be empowered to share with your grandchild a special person God created—you.

To Do with My Grandchild

Children love holidays, so designate a grandchild's half-birthday as a special event for just the two of you. Look for special foods that can be halved and still be delicious. For breakfast, serve pancakes or muffins cut in half. Lunch might be a variety of sandwich halves. For supper, offer meatballs cut in half before serving half a cake. Decorate with the correct number of candles, plus one very short candle. Surprise your grandchild with a complete present.

To Pray

Dear God,
There's so much in this world that I don't understand. Sometimes I feel limited in what I can offer others, or uncertain about ways I can contribute. Show me how to make a difference in the life of my grandchild. Amen.

To Reflect

A gift I can share with my grandchild is my...

_____

_____

_____

_____

_____

_____

_____

_____

_____

_____

_____

_____

_____

_____

_____

_____

_____

21

Be Brave

"Be strong and brave. Don't be afraid of them and don't be frightened,
because the LORD your God will go with you.
He will not leave you or forget you."

DEUTERONOMY 31:6

"Be brave."

That's what one grandma tells her grandchildren when saying good-bye. She doesn't only say, "See you soon," or "I love you." She adds, "Be brave." Initially, I thought that was an odd going-away message. After all, a child doesn't need courage to make it through the day. But this grandma is one wise woman.

A child might need courage to give a speech in the school auditorium. A child might need inner strength be bold enough to stand up to a playground bully. Even today, our grandchildren might be called on to look fear in the face.

The definition of bravery hasn't changed since David stood up to Goliath. A brave person still has the inner strength to face difficult or dangerous challenges. Our grandchildren live in a world with sharp, violent edges. Society won't always support our grandchild's Christian ethics and moral decisions. Even best buddies might question God-fearing choices. And yet we can sleep at night and wake up each morning, knowing that God is equipping our grandchildren to face their Goliaths. The words God spoke to Moses when he was 121 years old offer the same message God gives to our grandchildren of all ages: "Be strong and brave."

To Do with My Grandchild

Children naturally see David as a brave boy who faced the giant, so share stories of other, less familiar people in the Bible who were also courageous. Princess Michal helped her husband escape and bravely stood up to soldiers when they searched her house (1 Samuel 19:9–17). The Hebrew woman Jochebed was so brave that she floated her baby son down the Nile River in a basket to keep him safe (Exodus 2:1–10).

During your personal devotions, highlight other courageous people who can remind your grandchildren to "be strong and brave."

To Pray

Dear God,

As my grandchildren face Goliaths in their lives, empower them to embrace the words you gave to Moses: "Be strong and brave." Give them the courage to show the strength of character reflected by biblical heroes long ago. Through the years, help them build a strong moral core based on your teaching. Amen.

To Reflect

When I tell my grandchild about a biblical character who seemed brave…

_____

_____

_____

_____

_____

_____

_____

_____

_____

_____

_____

_____

_____

_____

_____

_____

_____

22

The Circle of Life

When they are old, they will still produce fruit;
they will be healthy and fresh.

PSALM 92:14

"Grandma's not old. She laughs."

I *did* laugh when I read this in an e-mail, which quoted our three-year-old grandson. But then I got serious. Does little Luke think people with gray hair don't have fun?

Stereotypes of older people saturate our youth-oriented culture. Media messages communicate that wrinkles demand plastic surgery, age spots are ugly, and all older people need to sit when taking a shower.

As grandmothers, we are older than others in the family. That's a fact. We might even be the oldest. Interacting with grandchildren is an effective way to combat the isolation, loneliness, and depression felt by some seniors.

Some older people feel a lack of purpose. They might wonder at their usefulness or the reason they are still alive. But regardless of our age, we have a specific agenda—to produce fruit for God. Nurturing a grandchild to grow up with Jesus gives us a deep purpose for living and a sense of direction for everything we do. Viewed through this lens, our age is a privilege, a true gift from God.

A healthy approach to growing older can be modeled by an elderly grandmother in a wheelchair or a fifty-something marathoner, because attitude—not age—forms the foundation of respect for the circle of life.

To Do with My Grandchild

Offsetting negative feelings about growing older can make a significant impact in a church congregation. Sponsoring cross-generational activities by matching grandchildren with our peers is one of many ways a church can show respect for life as a gift from God. Including mature Christians in mainstream ministries, not merely age-segmented activities, enhances and strengthens ministry for everyone.

Model a cross-age event by asking your grandchildren to invite their friends and their friends' grandmothers to your home or church for an ice cream social and root beer float party. Discuss other possible activities, trips, or experiences that could involve both grandchildren and their grandmothers.

To Pray

Dear God,
Thank you for the ability and health to continue as your servant. Guide me into areas of ministry that fulfill my desire to contribute and make a difference. May my attitude and activities reflect to you and others, including my grandchildren, the gratitude I feel for the years you have given me. Amen.

To Reflect

One way I can partner with my grandchild to bear fruit for the kingdom of God is...

23

Living Letters

You show that you are a letter from Christ sent through us.
This letter is not written with ink but with the Spirit of the living God.
It is not written on stone tablets but on human hearts.

2 CORINTHIANS 3:3

Updating a will to include a new grandchild, or even writing a will, becomes more urgent during the second half of life. But as Christians, we can bestow gifts on a grandchild long before we die. We give values long before we give valuables.

Each time we carry on a Christian family tradition, our grandchild sees how we prioritize family and honor those who have gone before us. When we attend church together, our grandchild sees how we grow in our relationship with God and connect with our faith community. When we volunteer at a local charity, we model Christian service.

Each action reflects our values, or something that is important to us. Regardless of whether or not we plan to leave a financial gift to a grandchild, researchers say that passing on spiritual and moral values gives grandparents a great deal of joy. St. Paul would say we become "living letters." As letters from Christ, we reflect His faithful love, a love that is always there. Even if grandchildren fall away from these Christian principles later in life or do not choose to embrace the values we share and model, we continue to be a living letter from Jesus.

To Do with My Grandchild

Research shows that as women become grandmothers, we often become more intentional about sharing values. You might include a preamble to your legal will that states the core Christian beliefs by which you lived. This can be read at a memorial service or other family gathering. Other grandmothers prepare a non-legal document called a "living inheritance." This spreadsheet matches values with specific action steps to insure core beliefs are shared with individual grandchildren. Action steps might include traditions, Bible stories, events, family heritage stories, or personal testimonies that support the values. Some action steps might involve other family members. This working document can be reviewed and revised annually as grandchildren grow up.

To Pray

Dear God,
Help me think about the ways I am a "living letter" from Christ. Give me new insights into the meaning of this concept, so that the love of Jesus comes through to the grandchildren I love. Amen.

To Reflect

Thinking of myself as a "living letter" from Christ to my grandchild...

_____

_____

_____

_____

_____

_____

_____

_____

_____

_____

_____

_____

_____

_____

_____

24

Discover Bonus Values

*All the Lord's followers often met together,
and they shared everything they had.*

ACTS 2:44 CEV

Sharing values is an important aspect of what we do as grandmothers. We weave faith, family, and friends into time with grandchildren.

But underneath the surface of those "big three" are values that rarely merit an asterisk on a list of core beliefs; we might not consider them significant either. After all, encouragement can't be compared to the all-important forgiveness, and yet Eunice and Lois are acknowledged as "encouragers of the faith" among women of the Bible (2 Timothy 1:5, 3:15). Artistic expression is minor when measured against courage, but Michal's creativity with goat hair and blankets gave her husband, David, time to escape capture by Saul's soldiers (1 Samuel 19:9–17). Every godly value, even if it appears "minor," is worth sharing with a grandchild.

During your personal devotions and Bible reading, actively seek to identify additional values that might be missed. Look for examples of teamwork, risk-taking, diversity, competence, and independence. Recall times when those "lesser" values contributed to good decisions or prevented mistakes. Discuss with your grandchild how additional virtues—justice, excellence, tolerance, and others—can become sources of strength.

Our willingness to discuss these values within the context of personal experience adds realness and authenticity. And like the new community of believers experienced in the Book of Acts, such heartfelt openness creates another bond between us and our grandchildren.

To Do with My Grandchild

We naturally fall into speech patterns that use familiar vocabulary. Just as you stretch values beyond the "big three" of faith, family, and friends, expand your language outside your usual terminology, as even the most attentive grandchild tunes out "same old, same old." Instead of saying, "Good job," when your grandchild presents artwork, say, "I love the way you mixed orange and pink to make a new color." Your grandchild will notice.

To Pray

Dear God,
Help my grandchild develop the breadth and depth of values that lead to becoming a contributing member of society. May both my grandchild and I model the biblical values that lead to moral choices and transform lives. Amen.

To Reflect

By building on a framework of faith, family, and friends, I can be most helpful to my grandchild when I...

_____

_____

_____

_____

_____

_____

_____

_____

_____

_____

_____

_____

_____

_____

25

The Peacemaker

"Blessed are the peacemakers, for they will be called children of God."

MATTHEW 5:9 NIV

If you've reserved the date, launched a webpage, created a logo for T-shirts, and booked a venue, your family might be ready for a reunion. As grandmothers, we often play a key role in organizing and making an event happen. But we might assume another less obvious role too—peacemaker.

As grandmothers, we prioritize relationships. Because we have lived longer than other family members, we have accumulated more history. We've heard all the stories about old arguments. We know who chooses topics that trigger intense emotions and which grandchildren tease each other. We can apply this wisdom to the event so that loved ones experience a sense of harmony at a family function and leave with good memories.

As followers of Jesus, we are not only instruments of peace, but are also called to seek opportunities for peace. That means we can be quick to thank a grandchild for setting the table. We can intervene with a tray of beverages before contestants in a lawn game have a heated exchange. Quite simply, we continue the same type of proactive engagement and Christian hospitality we practiced when we hosted our child's playgroup or birthday party years ago.

Being a peacemaker might be considered a minor element in grandmothering, but it's another way to leave faith footprints across the generations.

To Do with My Grandchild

A gathering is an ideal time to share family mission statements. The document can be detailed or brief, and include specific actions or only general principles. The content often includes values, goals, and priorities reflecting what's important to family members.

Individual family units can prepare the statements in advance and bring a printed copy or the framed copy that hangs in the home. This activity can be especially meaningful for those who have recently joined the extended family. Even though they are meeting a totally new group of people, they are on an equal footing when everyone brings a mission statement to share.

To Pray

Dear God,
Bless the times our family spends together. May each of us leave events and gatherings with a renewed sense of the many ways you have blessed us through the years. Amen.

To Reflect

Thinking of myself as a peacemaker...

26

Help Me Believe

The LORD God of Jacob blesses everyone
who trusts him and depends on him.

PSALM 146:5 CEV

How will my grandchildren turn out?

Even though they are growing up faster than our children did, it's too soon to tell if our grandchildren will become contributing members of society. Will they make wise choices? Have resilience to bounce back? Be respectful of others?

Of course, after years of being a mom, we know that lying awake worrying is a total waste of time. And as only one of many people who will influence this next generation, we won't get the blame or credit. But perhaps this lingering question about the future camouflages a deeper concern: Can I trust God with the grandchildren I love so much?

Even venturing to pose that question is almost frightening, for the level of trust mirrors our faith. After all, we believe the words of the psalmist. God has promised to bless "everyone who trusts him and depends on him." That's the message from our head. But can we really trust God with someone as precious as our grandchild? That's the question from our heart.

How can we be tempted to doubt our great God, who not only gave us the gift of children but this bonus blessing of grandchildren? Why do we even consider questioning Him?

Turning this issue over to God, we echo the words of that parent who so many years ago cried out to Jesus, "I do believe! Help me to believe more!" (Mark 9:24).

To Do with My Grandchild

Christian educators sometimes take children on a trust walk to demonstrate what it means to totally have faith in God. Blindfolded children are led through church hallways, completely dependent on their partners. You can duplicate that with a grandchild if you wish, but it's probably not necessary. Grandchildren already trust us to be there for them, to deliver what we promise, and most of all, to love them unconditionally. The relationship we've created with a grandchild, built on trust, parallels the relationship we have with God, doesn't it?

To Pray

Dear God,

Redirect any concern about my grandchild's future into a deepening faith in you. May my children and grandchildren have the confidence to trust your promises. Help me grow with them by embracing the future with hope. Amen.

To Reflect

Trusting God with my grandchild is...

27

Let's Celebrate!

"I the LORD do not change."

MALACHI 3:6 NIV

"*L*et's celebrate!"

Does your grandchild rate holidays by the number of presents or pieces of candy she receives? If so, Christmas and birthdays might rank at the top. But patriotic dates, which recognize an event that is important to our country, are also worth celebrating. Holiday rituals—whether it's hosting a cookout for relatives or waving a flag—become part of our family signature. Through the years and across the miles, traditions hold families together.

Historically, grandmothers have filled the role of "gatherer." And that's good, because we bring a long-term perspective. We've watched people enter and leave the family circle. We've seen some activities fade away while others become embedded into family lore. No one else might remember that the grandchildren decorate placemats for a meal or recall the best location to watch a parade.

Social scientists say that consistency is what makes family celebrations so enriching. Watching a grandchild grow up, literally before our eyes, reminds of us of the value of such predictability in a world of change. After all, sometimes we cling to empty traditions simply because the sameness feels comfortable.

Year after year, God is consistent. The Lord Himself speaks directly: "I the LORD do not change." Making Him a part of every family celebration is a worthy tradition to continue today and pass on to the next generation.

To Do with My Grandchild

Explore possible avenues of service that are developmentally appropriate for your grandchild. Help him identify personal passions. Most issues, even those on the world stage, are reflected in local agencies. Wildlife sanctuaries, animal shelters, and environmental agencies often appreciate people to work on campaigns in addition to helping with daily ongoing duties. When planning family gatherings, designate a time and opportunity that offers any family member the opportunity to volunteer. More participants will make a bigger impact on the charity and be a memorable event your grandchild might ask to repeat.

To Pray

Dear God,
Thank you for the overflowing goodness you continue to bring into my life: the gift of family, the reasons to celebrate, and the people who have gone before us to shape the family we love and the country in which we live. I am so grateful for your past blessings, the gifts you give today, and the promise of eternal life through your Son Jesus Christ. Amen.

To Reflect

A "good" family gathering is when...

_____

_____

_____

_____

_____

_____

_____

_____

_____

_____

_____

_____

_____

_____

_____

_____

_____

_____

_____

28

Power Up

Be on your guard and stay awake. Your enemy, the devil,
is like a roaring lion, sneaking around to find someone to attack.

1 Peter 5:8 CEV

"Look at my muscles, Grandma."

My grandson Josh regularly showcases his taut abs and impressive six-pack. His hard work is reflected in a strong core. Josh knows that all our movements—bending, standing, and even sitting—are powered by the core. While I'm delighted that he prioritizes physical fitness, I pray that he's also building a strong core as a Christian.

Every generation is challenged by temptations and issues unique to the times. Today, pop culture and societal influences are not only invasive, but also come with sometimes deadly consequences. Alternative paths can be enticing and attractive. Like us, our grandchildren need a strong core to resist and repel what the world offers.

If we strip down to the basics of what it means to be a spiritual mentor for a grandchild, we discover that the Holy Spirit empowers us from within. Our strength comes from the inside as God continually strengthens our core.

We can become even stronger when loved ones join our efforts to build spiritual muscles. Strengthening the core is serious business, spiritually and physically, but as grandmothers, we are power-packed women! Actions driven by a sturdy core can withstand the outside influences that threaten not only us, but also the grandchildren we cherish.

To Do with My Grandchild

Some people sum up their life in six words, or what's called a "life sentence." This often includes key words or actions that reflect a person's legacy. Tweak that tradition a bit to give your grandchild a life verse from the Bible. Ask God to lead you to a truth that will strengthen the child's spiritual core.

Some grandmothers vary the ritual and choose a new verse each year, often on the child's birthday. This verse can then be written, with the date, in a favorite Bible or Bible storybook.

To Pray

Dear God,
Many influences swirl around this child I love so much. Give my grandchild a strong Christian character to withstand the pressures and forces that threaten, now and in the future. Amen.

To Reflect

The "life sentence" I would choose today for my grandchild is…

_____

_____

_____

_____

_____

_____

_____

_____

_____

_____

_____

_____

_____

_____

_____

_____

29

Being Perfect

So be perfect, just as your Father in heaven is perfect.

MATTHEW 5:48 NIrV

I am not a perfect grandmother. That's hard to admit.

After years of attempting to be a perfect mom, I finally accepted the fact that I would never reach that goal. Now I face this pesky, recurring imperfection. I am not a perfect grandmother.

Have you ever whispered those words? You might spend more time with your grandchildren than I do. Many grandmas spend more money, and almost all grandmothers do more crafts with their grandchildren than I do. (At least, their masterpieces turn out better than mine!)

I don't like being imperfect at anything, especially when I try so hard. By saying, "Be perfect," Jesus sets the bar so high that I can never reach it. That hurts, because I hate to disappoint myself and others.

When I wallow in these depths, I need to reach for the lifeline of spiritual maturity. I grab on to the fact that Jesus came to do what I can't do. Only He can fix the imperfections I had as a mom. Only He can fill in the holes I have as a grandma.

When I go beyond myself to admit I need Jesus, I ache to hear good news. Actually, He has great news: I should try my best, but I don't need to reach perfection because He fills my place. Hallelujah!

To Do with My Grandchild

Does honesty rank at the top of your personal virtues? Being honest with ourselves isn't always easy, especially when focusing on important topics. Where does your grandchild rank honesty? When you're together, look for opportunities to link this virtue to what you see happening. Does he keep a promise? Acknowledge that. Say, "It's important to be truthful." Do you admit to making a mistake? Say, "It feels good to be honest." Drawing attention to core Christian values in everyday situations continually affirms and models making good choices.

To Pray

Dear God,
Thank you for Jesus, who fills in the empty places when I can't stretch far enough to reach the goal. Help me to continually come closer to the point of perfection at which I aim. I know you set the bar high so I can maximize the gifts you've given me. Thank you, God, for the blessings I know and the ones that are yet to come. Amen.

To Reflect

As a Christian woman, striving for perfection is a concept that...

30

Time in a Bottle

There is a time for everything, and a season
for every activity under the heavens.

ECCLESIASTES 3:1 NIV

Hit the pause button!

My grandchild is growing up too fast. Time is flying even more quickly than when I was raising a young one. During the awkward stages and difficult years of childrearing, I wanted to rush forward. I was afraid he'd never get out of diapers or learn to read. But now? I want to slow the pace. I yearn for more years of butterfly kisses and tight hugs from these little ones.

Honestly, though, it's not only my grandchild who is growing older too quickly. I am too. During the years of heavy-duty mothering, my kids were growing and developing, but I was too. Yet because the emphasis was always on them, I failed to acknowledge how changes over the years impacted me. Whoops! I forgot to look in the mirror. I was so busy being a mom that I lost sense of who I was and the "me" who was emerging.

Years ago, we couldn't hit the fast-forward button. Today, we can't click pause. Regardless of what we might think, the years are moving at precisely the right speed—God's speed. The Old Testament words are as true today as they were long before we gave birth to a child: "There is a time for everything, and a season for every activity under the heavens."

To Do with My Grandchild

Partner with your grandchild to make your personal "time in a bottle."

Remove the label from a clean empty bottle with a neck of at least one inch in diameter. Substitute a tall, narrow transparent plastic container if working with a young child. Layer one inch of sandbox sand, white sugar, or salt in the bottom. (You will use more of this same "filler" throughout the project.)

Each time you are with your grandchild during the next weeks or months, add a layer of small objects related to something you did or a holiday you experienced together. For example, use candy hearts for Valentine's Day; red, white, and blue confetti if you watched a parade; shiny pennies if you went shopping, etc. Add a thicker layer of objects than you think necessary, because the filler you add between layers of objects will press down your objects over time. Store the bottle in a safe place (i.e., where a child cannot shake it).

When the bottle is full, your grandchild can glue on craft jewels to make a cross as a reminder of the many ways God blessed your time together.

To Pray

Dear God,
I am so grateful for the time with my grandchild. I am so grateful for this precious gift. Thank you. Amen.

To Reflect

Knowing that my grandchild and I both live according to God's timeframe...

_____

_____

_____

_____

_____

_____

_____

_____

_____

_____

_____

_____

_____

_____

_____

31

Dig Deep

Until I come, spend your time reading Scripture out loud to one another.
Spend your time preaching and teaching.

1 TIMOTHY 4:13 NIrV

Many grandmothers find that sharing Bible stories with grandchildren becomes a treasured activity. When a grandchild scurries off to get the "God book" for you, it's obvious you've left a faith footprint. Life doesn't get much better than when we hold an open Bible storybook and a grandchild. That's a moment to savor.

But we can build on the close relationship we have with our grandchildren, to introduce them to biblical heroes beyond the obvious David, Moses, and Noah. The episode that takes place when St. Paul preaches an overly long sermon in an upper room, cloudy with smoke from oily pots (Acts 9:22–25), might never make the list of top ten favorites, but it's a hidden treasure worth sharing.

Our grandchildren are growing up at a time when authenticity oozes from advertisements, social media, and pop culture. The desire for realness has become a defining characteristic for the generations that follow us. A grandchild who hears about the young boy who falls asleep while St. Paul preaches nonstop for hours, might want to learn about other interesting people in the Bible.

Sharing the story of Judge Deborah (Judges 4:4–16) or Elisha and the poisoned pot of stew (2 Kings 4:38–41) not only expands a child's level of biblical literacy, but also contributes to your own spiritual growth.

And isn't that what often happens? When we have a pure and honest intention to help our grandchild grow, we grow too.

To Do with My Grandchild

When doing your personal Bible reading and devotions, use a blank piece of paper as a bookmark. Then as you read, start listing little-known Bible stories to share with your grandchild. Consider stories like The Busy Housekeeper (Luke 11:38–42), Down in the Well (Jeremiah 38:1–13), Mister Moneybags (Mark 2:13–14), and X Marks the Spot (2 Kings 6:8–23). Some of these episodes are very short. As you tell the story, paint rich word pictures so your grandchild can visualize the scenes and characters.

To Pray

Dear God,

I am often surprised at what I discover in the Bible. Even in a familiar section, the Holy Spirit will suddenly give me an unexpected insight or fresh perspective. Thank you for the opportunity to share this excitement and energy for your Word with my grandchild. Amen.

To Reflect

The first time I shared my favorite Bible story with my grandchild...

32

A Next-Gen Grand?

Whatever you do, do all to the glory of God.
1 Corinthians 10:31 NKJV

Trend-spotters highlight innovation and change, but how much do societal swings and shifts influence your grandmothering? In other words, are you a Next-Gen Grand?

Digital communication touches everyone to some degree. This requires us to be proactive in knowing family rules regarding technology. Is a visiting toddler allowed to play with your tablet? Can an eight-year-old carry his phone on a shopping trip with you? Respecting parental guidelines has real-time urgency as unfiltered content reaches even young grandchildren.

In a world where a grandchild's social status can be determined by his number of online friends, we might wonder if our Christian traditions and family values have lost relevance. But "new" does not define what's good; faster is not necessarily better. When time moves at hyper speed, what's familiar and recognizable takes on added significance.

Knowing that Christians through the centuries have used the prayer Jesus taught gives a sense of well-being as we repeat the same words with our grandchild (Matthew 6: 9–13). We might teach grandchildren to sing a mealtime prayer as the disciples did after the Last Supper (Matthew 26:30). Personal family history might be reflected in words you prayed with your children and now share with the next generation.

When we live according to the words of St. Paul and "do all the glory of God," trendiness isn't the yardstick.

To Do with My Grandchild

Partner with your grandchild to make a family prayer book. Include prayers you said as a child, prayers you taught your children, and prayers your grandchild uses now. Your grandchild might want to illustrate the pages or use an online design program to lay out the pages. Use it as a birthday gift for family members.

To Pray

Dear God,

Over the years, I've shared so many burdens with you, and many joys too. I'm just grateful you don't get tired of listening. My prayer today is for my grandchild. Help this precious child to pray with confidence, knowing you will never tire of hearing her voice. Amen.

To Reflect

I want to help my grandchild view prayer as...

_____

_____

_____

_____

_____

_____

_____

_____

_____

_____

_____

_____

_____

_____

_____

_____

_____

_____

33

Accelerate!

You must be very careful not to forget the things you have seen God do for you.
Keep reminding yourselves, and tell your children and grandchildren as well.

DEUTERONOMY 4:9 CEV

Have you retrained your brain to be a grandmother?

That's not such a crazy question. As moms, we spend years drowning in backpacks and soccer practice, worrying about bullies and school lunches. As grandmothers, we can let the worry go. Really, let it go! Simply concentrate on what matters. And for starters, fun matters.

We can hand over the baby who needs a new diaper. We leave before the bedtime bath chaos erupts. We go home to celebrate the quiet because we've earned an early exit from the daily grind. As grandmothers, we can be more relaxed and easygoing, which makes life more fun.

But years ago, we lectured our children that freedom comes with responsibilities. We can't escape that truth just because we're now grandmothers. The freedom to have fun with children, without the exhaustion of parenting, is accompanied by a sense of urgency about our responsibility.

Sharing the Word of God was part of our job description as parents. But as grandmothers, we are more aware of the timeframe. A simple game of tag with grandchildren, which leaves us panting and tired, reminds us that we don't have forever.

Moses prompts us to remember that we have experienced God's power and received His blessings. It's time to accelerate the sharing of that message with grandchildren.

To Do with My Grandchild

Scripture does not change, but increasing the fun factor in delivering the content can make a big difference to a child. Share a devotional under a tent (a sheet thrown across two chairs works well). Play Bible-based games together, online or offline. Or simply ask your grandchild, "Where should we read the Bible today?" Reinforce the fact that growing up as a child of God can be fun.

To Pray

Dear God,
Thank you for the gift of time to share with grandchildren. May I use this time wisely to teach them how to live as your children and share your love with others. Amen.

To Reflect

I am confident that God blesses the time I spend with my grandchild because...

_____

_____

_____

_____

_____

_____

_____

_____

_____

_____

_____

_____

_____

_____

_____

34

Exceeding Expectations

I don't do the good things I want to do.
I keep on doing the evil things I don't want to do.

ROMANS 7:19 NIrV

Buy more insect repellant. Wash off soap bubbles a grandchild spilled on the driveway. Wipe fingerprints off the windows. It's easy to feel like we're on rewind when life as a grandmother doesn't seem much different from life as a mom. When expectations clash with reality, disappointment magnifies. Energy spirals downward.

Sometimes that happens with our spiritual walk too. When we neglect the opportunity to invite someone to worship or when we listen to gossip in a conversation, we're reduced to floundering as a limp Christian.

But it's even more difficult to forgive ourselves when we fail to help a grandchild move closer to Christ. We might not feel any better knowing that St. Paul experienced a similar struggle. After all, he described the situation perfectly: "I don't do the good things I want to do. I keep on doing the evil things I don't want to do."

How can being a Christian grandmother be so tough? Sharing our love of Jesus with the grandchild we love should be easy. Yet we don't always grab the opportunities or maximize the occasion.

God might use this "expectations vs. reality" struggle as a teachable moment. Even a Christian grandma might need to be reminded of how much we need our Savior. Only He will exceed our expectations.

To Do with My Grandchild

Teachable moments can occur when we say to a grandchild, "Let's snuggle up with the Bible and read together." But the Holy Spirit can also work through indirect everyday situations. Your grandchild might talk about a difficult situation at school while you're folding clothes together or walking the dog. Staying alert for uncommon moments when we can share biblical truths will help us maximize those opportunities.

To Pray

Dear God,
One way I show how much you mean to me is by sharing your Word. Open my eyes to see the opportunities. Equip me with the words to say. Empower me with the confidence to talk about the many ways you are actively involved in everyday situations. Amen.

To Reflect

It is easy to tell my grandchild about Jesus when...

35

Sweet Dreams

I can lie down and sleep soundly because you, LORD, will keep me safe.
PSALM 4:8 CEV

I'd love to protect my grandchildren from bad dreams. Although I wrap my arms around them when I hear them cry in the dark, I ache to shield them from the scary thoughts and images that startle them while sleeping. Unfortunately, not even a grandma's love can protect these precious children from everything.

When shadows invade their thoughts and minds, sharing Scripture can be incredibly comforting. Even a preschooler can whisper the words with us, again and again, "I can lie down and sleep soundly because you, LORD, will keep me safe." Accompanying the verse with a gentle backrub or a sip of water can help.

Families often include making a shadow cross as part of the regular bedtime ritual. Show your grandchild how to make the shape of a cross, using a finger from each hand. When the lights are turned off, the cross will appear as a shadow on the wall. Bad dreams increase when a child is worried or stressed, such as the night before school begins or before a medical appointment. Teaching how to make this simple finger cross can be especially beneficial at these times. Seeing the cross is a visual reminder that the child can repeat the comforting Scripture verse whenever she's scared at night.

As we age, many of us find it harder to get to sleep or stay asleep. Repeating the words of the psalmist might be helpful for us too.

To Do with My Grandchild

Ask your adult child to recall the bedtime routine used during childhood. Usually, our children will recall exactly what we did and in what order teeth were brushed and prayers were said. During a conversation in which we revisit these bedtime routines, it becomes obvious how valuable these rituals were in their life. Often, the pattern used years ago will be repeated with our grandchild.

To Pray

Dear God,
Please keep my grandchild in the palm of your hand as he sleeps at night. May her nights be filled with peaceful dreams so she awakes refreshed for the new day. Amen.

To Reflect

I know my grandchild is afraid of something when...

36

What's in a Name?

I have called you by name, and you are mine.

ISAIAH 43:1

Whether we respond to Granny, Mimi, or NanaBanana, we are grandmothers. Regardless of the term, our name is a symbol of endearment. In biblical times, a name reflected character or told something about a person. God bluntly told Moses, "I am who I am" (Exodus 3:14 NIV).

Although a child's naming rights clearly belong to the parents, some grandmas lobby for a namesake or campaign for a "proper" name. Others hope to continue the legacy of a family member through the name of a grandchild.

You might remember that the naming of a child is a deeply personal experience. As expectant moms years ago, we might have scribbled potential names for a child on the back of an envelope. When naming our grandchild, our adult children might have downloaded lengthy lists of trendy, ethnic, celebrity, and eco-friendly children's names before creating an even more unique name.

When we see our bald elderly cousin Fuzzy, or six-feet five-inch "Junior," we are reminded that names and nicknames last a lifetime. However, the "grand" in grandparent can be tarnished very quickly if we comment negatively on the choice of a grandchild's name.

Regardless of the name on a birth certificate, being called God's child is most important. We can rejoice across the generations that God says to all of us, "I have called you by your name. You are mine" (Isaiah 43:1 NKJV).

To Do with My Grandchild

With your grandchild, trace the history of his name; find out why his name was chosen. Then use an online dictionary to look up the meaning of the middle names for both you and your grandchild. Do your names match your personalities? Also research the names of favorite Bible heroes. Do those names match their personalities?

To Pray

Dear God,
Thank you for welcoming both my grandchild and me into your family. My heart overflows with gratitude, knowing that you have called us by name and claimed us as your own. Amen.

To Reflect

When someone says "grandmother," the first thing I think about is...

_____

_____

_____

_____

_____

_____

_____

_____

_____

_____

_____

_____

_____

_____

_____

_____

_____

37

The "Lois Challenge"

I am reminded of your sincere faith, which first lived in your grandmother Lois and in your mother Eunice and, I am persuaded, now lives in you also.

2 TIMOTHY 1:5 NIV

The biblical hero Lois must have been an amazing person. Of all the godly women in the Bible who were grandmothers—others being Sarah, Rebecca, Rachel, and Ruth—Lois is the only woman called grandmother. St. Paul notes she had a "sincere" faith. Other biblical scholars translate her faith as "genuine" or "honest." Regardless of the specific adjective, Lois modeled a real, relatable faith.

Our grandchildren need to see a Lois-level authenticity from us. Their generation is growing up at a time when transparency is valued. Honest communication cuts through the clutter. Communication from the heart connects at a deeper level than a mere exchange of information or news. So how can we become a contemporary Lois?

We start by reading and studying Scripture. The biblical Lois did that with her grandson, Timothy. The biblical Lois was also an encourager in the Christian faith for her daughter, Eunice. We can assume that role for our adult child.

A modern Lois might volunteer to read to children at the library, join a walk for the hungry, or participate in causes that support the environment. Whatever the activity, in Bible times or today, a grandmother with "sincere faith" would demonstrate faith in action.

You and I have a grandchild. We are women of faith. Let's embrace the "Lois Challenge" and model a "sincere faith" for the next generation.

To Do with My Grandchild

With geographic gaps between families, your grandchildren, like mine, might live halfway across the country. Even if you're blessed by living near family members, spheres of daily living might rarely connect.

Before the next face time with your grandchild, prioritize personal core virtues. What matters the most? Honesty? Kindness? Patience? Forgiveness? Then the next time you are with your grandchild, look for opportunities to live out that virtue. Actions naturally follow beliefs, so if patience or forgiveness is your priority, your grandchild will naturally observe and experience that virtue. Even with children who live in cyberspace, actions speak louder than words.

To Pray

Dear God,

Empower my personal character to become stronger and more sincere in faith. Help me maximize opportunities to put my Christian beliefs into action. I long to have my grandchild know you and love you as deeply as I do. Please continue to direct our paths and guide our faith journeys. Amen.

To Reflect

A "sincere faith" includes...

_____

_____

_____

_____

_____

_____

_____

_____

_____

_____

_____

_____

_____

_____

_____

_____

_____

_____

38

Tech Talks

Seek good and not evil.
Amos 5:14 NKJV

Technology can be a great connector. Skype, e-mail, online gaming, and social media platforms can bring us closer to a grandchild. Our skills might be limited, but even a young grandchild can usually solve any cyber issue. Grandchildren are amused and affirmed when they can teach us.

But we face the same digital dangers that threaten our grandchildren. Preventing tech addiction and avoiding offensive online content require continued vigilance. Technology can be so seductive; we might be challenged to find a healthy balance between real life and virtual space.

Screens can even impact the ability to make eye contact and read body language. Informally test yourself and your grandchild. Can you look steadily into your grandchild's eyes for the duration of a one-minute conversation? Can you and your grandchild read each other's body language? These fun and simple assessments can be informative.

The Old Testament prophet Amos didn't caution the people of Israel about the lure of modern technology, but he stated an instruction that cuts across time: "Seek good and not evil." That's basic, and the direction works as well today as it did years ago.

Modern technology multiplies the number of attractive and available choices, but even the most dynamic high-tech invention will not change our healthy response: "Seek good, not evil."

To Do with My Grandchild

Use technology to bring your grandchild closer to you and to God. Invite your grandchild to take photos with a phone or tablet as you walk through a park or nature preserve. Even a very young child will find it easy to click the button. As you walk, draw attention to the many wonders of God's creation by looking at small details that might be missed with only a quick glance. Work with an older child to add Bible verses to photos that can be shared online with relatives. (If you don't know how to do this, just ask. Your grandchild probably knows how to do it.) Although references to God's creation are found throughout Scripture, look especially at Psalms 24, 65, 104, 147, and 148 for rich imagery. Using technology alongside your grandchild adds one more way you can connect across generations.

To Pray

Dear God,

Help me to make wise choices about technology. May I develop the skills that lead me to effectively communicate, create, and connect. As options and alternatives multiply, lead both my grandchild and me to seek good and not evil. Amen.

To Reflect

Watching my grandchild use technology, I...

_____

_____

_____

_____

_____

_____

_____

_____

_____

_____

_____

_____

_____

_____

_____

_____

39

Transitions

The LORD himself will go before you. He will be with you;
he will not leave you or forget you. Don't be afraid and don't worry.

DEUTERONOMY 31:8

Transitions are a part of everyday life—literally!

From waking up in the morning to going to bed at night, we move from one place to another, from one role to another. Most shifts are seamless.

Waving goodbye to grandchildren is not always as easy. We might put on a cheerful face until the door closes, then dissolve into tears. Even if we don't feel the separation as acutely, adjusting to a "new normal" without the chatter of little voices can take time. Soon, though, we're back to our usual routine, blowing kisses into Skype.

Transitions can be hard on our grandchildren too. After time apart, they might need to get reacquainted with us or re-learn to read our visual cues. Bringing a new book to read or ingredients to make a favorite snack can help to bridge the gap for everyone.

Life-changing transitions that impact us can also impact our grandchildren. The death of a pet that always eased the awkward first moments of a visit, leaves an emptiness. Our downsizing from a big house might mean there isn't space for sleepovers. At these times, we draw from the depth of our relationships, depend on established patterns, and request God's presence.

During tough transitions, allow yourself to lean into God. That's His hand on your shoulder.

To Do with My Grandchild

Bridge transitions between grandchild visits by sharing video clips, mementos, or photos from a previous visit. Recalling good times will remind grandchildren of the fun you've had in the past and help them anticipate time together in the future.

To Pray

Dear God,
Help me to trust your promises during times of uncertainty or change. May our increased dependence on you reflect a growth in the faith my grandchild and I share in your promises. Amen.

To Reflect

During a transition, I can be especially helpful to my grandchild…

_____

_____

_____

_____

_____

_____

_____

_____

_____

_____

_____

_____

_____

_____

_____

_____

_____

40

A Bucket List

This is the day that the L\ord has made. Let us rejoice and be glad today!

PSALM 118:24

Making a bucket list can be exciting and depressing. It's encouraging to think of all we can do, but distressing when we consider our age. However, writing a variation of a bucket list with a grandchild is a completely uplifting experience when done in the spirit of the psalmist's words: "This is the day that the L\ord has made. Let us rejoice and be glad today!"

God has given us today. He has given us a grandchild. In what ways can we celebrate this gift of time together?

With a young child, you might start by saying, "What can we do today?" Young children are realistic and live in the moment. They will glance around, see a rake, and say, "We can rake leaves." Slightly older children view a bucket list as a convenient way to get everything on a wish list. They often need redirecting to think of experiences the two of you could share. Older grandchildren easily generate so many great (and sometimes wild) ideas that you might end up substituting "Ride in a hot air balloon" with "Drop water balloons from the deck."

Checking off items on a bucket list with a grandchild connects two of God's most valuable gifts: creativity and time. Or, using the words of the psalmist, "Let us rejoice and be glad today!"

To Do with My Grandchild

Making time count with a grandchild does not require money or extensive plans. Even an older grandchild is often interested in how we spend our day. If a child helps water the plants or vacuums during one visit, the next time she will ask, "Do the plants need watering, Grandma?" Do something once with a child, and a tradition is born.

Consider simple activities, like painting a large stone to make a tic-tac-toe board, weaving clover flowers to make a crown, or shopping at a local thrift store. Regardless of what you do, time with a grandchild is always a good investment of God's gifts.

To Pray

Dear God,
I so appreciate the time I have with my grandchild. May I model wise use of our hours together and take every opportunity to help her grow in knowing you better. Amen.

To Reflect

The next time my grandchild and I are together...

41
Lifelong Learning

Teach the wise, and they will become even wiser;
teach good people, and they will learn even more.

PROVERBS 9:9

What has surprised you most about having a grandchild? For me, I've been amazed at how much I continue to learn. When I finally figure out one feature on a new phone, I'm reminded that I still have things to learn. Perhaps it's this continuing sense of discovery that makes each day with a grandchild so interesting.

When I can't figure out technology, I look to my youngest grandchild. Often, this same expert on all things digital also offers a pure, uncomplicated perspective on faith-related topics. I wonder how young children can be so insightful. After all, they can't draw from the same lifetime of experiences that make us so brilliant. Yet these children observe, listen, and learn.

They help us bake cookies for a new mom. They plunge their hands into disposable gloves to sort clothes with us at the thrift shop. And a grandchild who sees my favorite Bible marked with a rainbow of Post-it Notes, correctly concludes that I am still learning too.

I tend to adopt an air of religious superiority when I do something that's related to spiritual nurture. I feel almost saint-like wrapping a new Bible storybook. But perhaps if I paid less attention to what I do and more attention to how the Holy Spirit uses everyday actions, my grandchild, and especially I, would grow wiser.

To Do with My Grandchild

Children learn best through play. Because grandmothers are experts at having fun, it makes sense to play through Bible stories with grandchildren. Perhaps you and your grandchild act out a favorite story for the family, complete with scarf-turbans and beach-towel tunics. Or, you challenge an older grandchild to tell a Bible story using various forms of poetry like haiku or limericks. How many ways can you mix Bible learning with fun for your grandchild?

To Pray

Dear God,

As our world keeps changing, I realize that I need to continue learning. Help me share with my grandchild the joy I feel when I learn more about you. Amen.

To Reflect

To help my grandchild experience joy in learning more about Jesus Christ, I...

_____

_____

_____

_____

_____

_____

_____

_____

_____

_____

_____

_____

_____

_____

_____

_____

42

Dinner is Served

Let each of you look out not only for his own interests,
but also for the interests of others.

PHILIPPIANS 2:4 NKJV

Have you noticed? The family dinner has disappeared.

Although gathering for supper provides an ideal time to share values, learn manners, and engage in meaningful conversation, only a limited number of grandchildren are sitting at the table. Extracurricular activities, an accelerated pace of life, and our snacking culture have contributed to the empty seats.

Realistically, we won't change the direction of society; however, we can still make a difference at the table. Hosting family dinner (or brunch, lunch, or a picnic) can be one example of how we fit into our grandchildren's world. We prioritize what's important to us as grandmothers, and then slip those elements into the moving pieces that make up modern life.

Food has been a connector across generations, so even now, time in the kitchen can be a building block for relationships. The current trend toward personalized eating means that multiple dishes are served at the same meal. Perhaps this means your grandchild takes "orders" in advance and then you both prepare the food. Or, when you grocery shop together, you promise your grandchild half of the money saved by couponing.

Actively seeking ways to connect cross-generationally against a background of today's fluid family helps us live out the Scriptural principle: "Let each of you look out not only for his own interests, but also for the interests of others."

To Do with My Grandchild

Depend on grandchildren to keep you current. They might not know what to call the move from processed to organic, but they'll know that Mommy "only buys food with ingredients I can pronounce." Seeing trends through the eyes of a grandchild helps us avoid cross-generational stumbles and allows us to offer realistic help.

To Pray

Dear God,
I can barely keep up with what's happening in my tiny corner or the world, yet you keep the universe spinning. You amaze me every day. I thank you. I praise you. May I honor you with ways I serve. Amen.

To Reflect

My grandchild helps me...

_____

_____

_____

_____

_____

_____

_____

_____

_____

_____

_____

_____

_____

_____

_____

_____

_____

_____

43

Marching Orders

On your feet wear the Good News of peace to help you stand strong.

EPHESIANS 6:15

Ballet slippers, soccer shoes with cleats, sandals, snow boots. We couldn't seem to keep them sorted or even paired together when our kids were growing up. And the cost! If you've gifted your grandchild with footwear recently, you've probably noticed that the price of children's shoes (even soft-soled infant shoes) has skyrocketed.

As Christians equipped to stand against the Devil, we wear special shoes. When describing the whole armor of God, St. Paul uses imagery from a Roman soldier. The sole of his sandal was studded with sharp nails. These cleats gave the soldier a solid footing on any surface. Wearing God's sandals prepares us to share the gospel at a moment's notice; we are foot soldiers ready for the task, wherever we are called.

Sometimes I don't want to go where God leads. I'm content in my cozy little corner of the world; give me a grandchild to snuggle and I'm set. And yet, that carefree existence isn't the life to which you or I have been called. We need to venture out into a scary world that craves the peace, love, and salvation that only Jesus offers.

I don't know the dangers my grandchildren or I will face in the future. I can't imagine what waits ahead, but suited in the whole armor of God, my loved ones and I can step out with boldness and confidence.

To Do with My Grandchild

Give your grandchild a map and marker to track the route to your house, church, or school. A young child only has a generalized sense of time and space, but around the age of seven or eight, she begins to understand spatial relationships. Or, put on your walking shoes and print an aerial view of your neighborhood. Mark a route you can walk together. Even if she can't follow the map, offering this type of real-time practice adds a depth of meaning to her academic learning. This activity also demonstrates your willingness to support her overall development and not only her spiritual growth.

To Pray

Dear God,
I believe my grandchild and I are ready, willing, and able to go where you lead. Equip us with what we need to do your work in the ways you intend. Help us navigate the path as we follow you. Amen.

To Reflect

I can help my grandchild feel equipped and empowered to face the future by...

_____

_____

_____

_____

_____

_____

_____

_____

_____

_____

_____

_____

_____

_____

_____

44

Thanksgiving Everyday

*Let us come before him with thanksgiving
and extol him with music and song.*

PSALM 95:2 NIV

Although Americans sometimes claim Thanksgiving as their holiday, harvest events are as old as the Bible. In the Book of Leviticus, we read that the Feast of Booths highlighted both the harvest and Israel's forty-year journey on the Exodus. During the feast, people lived in tents to remind themselves of God's provision during their sojourn.

Today, harvest traditions vary around the globe. Common themes are harmony, thanks, and gratitude for the harvest. In the United Kingdom, home-grown produce is used to decorate churches in September. In Australia, the March event celebrates the grape and apple harvest and features celebrity grape crushing and various apple competitions.

As Christians, we can live each day as if it were Thanksgiving. Many of us begin and end each day with thanks to God for our grandchildren. Periodically reminding them of this prayer cover provides a natural opportunity to ask, "Do you have specific needs I can pray for?" Knowing that we have their backs deepens the level of spiritual engagement with grandchildren.

Beginning each day with a praise prayer helps us keep other issues in perspective. We might grumble about the way holiday plans seem to be working out or express concern about hosting an upcoming family event, but those matters fade when we focus on the blessing of being a grandmother.

To Do with My Grandchild

As you anticipate celebrating holiday traditions, consider adding ways that family members of all ages can focus on God's blessings. Even young children can be involved in a Bible pass-around. As the family Bible passes from person to person, each one reading a verse from Psalm 148, young children clap each time they hear the phrase "Praise the Lord." Or, everyone repeats the phrase "For His mercy endures forever" each time it appears in Psalm 136. Unifying the family around Scripture always gives another reason to thank God.

To Pray

Dear God,
I want to shout for joy and offer heartfelt praise for my grandchildren. They are such blessings to me. Today let my gratitude for your goodness be reflected in what I say and do. Amen.

To Reflect

When I show my gratitude to God by trying to be like Jesus...

45

Pass It On

Jesus Christ is the same yesterday and today and forever.
HEBREWS 13:8 NIV

Saying no wasn't easy when we had young children. Saying no still isn't easy.

After all, we don't want the reputation of being the grandma who says, "No cookies before supper," or "No staying up any later." But when fundraising grandkids ask us to buy another tin of popcorn, the tenth box of cookies, or still more wrapping paper, saying no might become necessary. Like so many situations in our mothering, we face multiple judgment calls as a grandmother.

Today, though, decisions are based on applying what we've learned after years of raising children. Staying alert to trends, research, and new ideas will impact what we do with grandchildren, because we remember the age-old proverb: Experience isn't the best teacher; learning from experience is the best teacher.

As well, the "doubling curve" has changed so dramatically that general knowledge doubles every twelve months. Obviously, the right judgment call years ago might not be the correct response today.

That's why it's comforting to know that the basics don't change. We can pass on to our grandchildren the same virtues we taught our children. We can worship with grandchildren in the same church that our children attended. We can read to our grandchildren the same reassuring words from Hebrews that our children heard: "Jesus Christ is the same yesterday and today and forever." We pray that they will also pass it on.

To Do with My Grandchild

Research shows that tech-savvy children tend to be impatient; after all, everything moves more quickly in virtual space than in real time. Does your grandchild wait patiently for you to finish a sentence? Does he have the social listening skill to be patient when you pause to think? Choose a favorite story in the Bible. Then, read one verse and have your grandchild read the next. Alternating verses in this way increases literacy, reinforces social listening skills, and shares the Good News.

To Pray

Dear God,

Thank you for giving us the Bible. As I share this treasure with my grandchild, help us both increase our knowledge and understanding of your will for our lives. Amen.

To Reflect

Those who help my grandchild learn about God...

_____

_____

_____

_____

_____

_____

_____

_____

_____

_____

_____

_____

_____

_____

_____

_____

_____

_____

46
Love Notes

Children are a gift from the LORD. They are a reward from him.

PSALM 127:3 NIrV

*C*ongratulations!

The arrival of a new grandchild is a blessing from God. This new life will not only deepen a family legacy by continuing your heritage, but this child is also a continuation of God's own creation. That is all worth celebrating.

But stay alert. Satan prowls around this happy scene. Sin can spark comparisons ("She gave us diapers but bought them a crib"), jealousy ("Why does she always go there for Thanksgiving?"), and even snide remarks among our own children ("Don't be so possessive of Mom.")

If this happens, we will need to work hard to stay focused on this new love gift from God. We will need His help to turn away from situations or conversations that threaten to tarnish the joy. This is especially true if we gain several grandchildren at the same time or add step-grandkids to the family. These children offer more reasons to celebrate, but also the potential for more complex relationships.

A new grandchild allows us to "pay forward" the Christian virtues and core beliefs we treasure. What an opportunity! The psalmist reminds us this new child is not only a "gift" but a "reward." As grateful grandmothers, we join with the holy writer to "Give thanks to the LORD because he is good. His love continues forever" (Psalm 136:1).

To Do with My Grandchild

The addition of a grandchild offers an opportunity to begin a new tradition that can span the years. Each year, on the child's birthday or the anniversary of the day the child was adopted or entered the family through foster care ("Welcome Day" or "Gotcha Day"), write a letter to your grandchild. Content might vary through the years, but include moments you have shared a special closeness with God and each other. Drop the note into a larger envelope if you want to add tickets, artwork, letters, or mementos from the past twelve months. Clearly label each envelope with the year. Give the box of love notes to your grandchild on a milestone birthday.

To Pray

Dear God,
Fill my heart with the deep joy and thanksgiving brought by the special love gift from you—a new grandchild. May our family welcome this child as a continuation of your creation. Amen.

To Reflect

Knowing that my grandchild is a gift from God to our family means...

_____

_____

_____

_____

_____

_____

_____

_____

_____

_____

_____

_____

_____

_____

_____

_____

_____

_____

47

Give Thanks

Give thanks to the Lord, because he is good.
His faithful love continues forever.

PSALM 136:1 NIrV

*C*an you smell the memories?

During autumn, our sense of smell comes alive as feel-good aromas emanate from the kitchen. Scientists say that happens because floating molecules meet our neurons, but even the most complex equation can't capture the vintage memories that wake up when pumpkin pie, turkey, and roasted squash cram the oven.

Joining with family members to feast, watch football, or shop can be a centerpiece for any gathering. Even if we sit with a grandchild to compile only a short list of blessings, the psalmist reminds us that God is good. More than that, He is faithful. We can always count on Him to be dependable, trustworthy, and reliable. Sometimes even cherished loved ones can't claim those character traits.

A two-year-old grandchild who learns to say thank you has reached a moral milestone. For all of us, expressing gratitude to God not only for His blessings, but also for His faithfulness, leads to a feeling of hope. That was true in Bible times, and is also true today.

St. Luke records the story of the ten lepers (Luke 17:11–19). Jesus healed them all, but only one came back to say thank you. Those two words sound so simple, but they offer a direct way to focus on the goodness we receive from our ever-faithful God.

To Do with My Grandchild

Expand your grandchild's appreciation of the tremendous variety in God's cornucopia, by welcoming her to the kitchen. A young child is a concrete learner who learns by tasting, touching, smelling, and seeing foods at various stages of preparation. When older grandchildren graduate from helping you mix and measure ingredients in an heirloom recipe, involve them by filming a video clip. "Behind the Scenes in Grandma's Kitchen" will be a hit at your next family gathering.

To Pray

Dear God,

As I remember your generosity, may I more consistently express thanks. Sometimes I get so caught up enjoying those blessings that I forget to say thank you. Help me celebrate your goodness. Amen.

To Reflect

Saying thank you seems like a little thing, but...

_____

_____

_____

_____

_____

_____

_____

_____

_____

_____

_____

_____

_____

_____

_____

_____

_____

_____

_____

_____

48

More than Money

God loves people who love to give.
2 Corinthians 9:7 CEV

As members of the "grandparent economy," you and I belong to a powerful group. Even if we count pennies and carefully manage every financial asset, we still reflect a wealthy generation.

Perhaps like you, I enjoy buying gifts. It feels good to be generous. Long before Christmas, I anticipate the joy that holiday presents will bring. But especially as we near the holidays, it's easy to go overboard. In our consumer-focused world, commercial messages scream "more is better." However, that's not always true. Giving more presents than the "other" grandmother doesn't mean we are a "better" grandma.

St. Paul reminds the people of Corinth (and us too) that "God loves people who love to give." That generosity includes sharing all of God's blessings: our time, talents, and treasures. During the coming weeks, our most meaningful gift might not be tied with a big red bow. Instead, we might care for a sick child so a parent can attend a school program or be the specified adult while a teen practices driving. Our time is a gift.

When we consider sharing all of God's blessings, the opportunities to be generous extend far beyond the current grandparent economy. We can give confidently from an overflowing heart, for we are assured that, "You will be blessed in every way and you will be able to keep on being generous" (2 Corinthians 9:11 CEV).

To Do with My Grandchild

"Togethering," or making an emotional connection, is at the heart of grandmothering. We've learned through experience that being intentional, not incidental, about spending time with loved ones, is one of God's greatest blessings.

Recall your best togethering moments with your grandchild. Identify what made that time so memorable. Was it the amount of time? What you were doing? Your preparation for the visit? Attempt to duplicate some of those elements during a future visit.

To Pray

Dear God,
During this holiday season, broaden my vision beyond "things" to give generously of myself. May I share the variety of gifts you give me, permitting others to be blessed in ways I might not even imagine. Amen.

To Reflect

I see God's generosity...

_____

_____

_____

_____

_____

_____

_____

_____

_____

_____

_____

_____

_____

_____

_____

_____

_____

_____

49

Kids in the Kitchen

The believers met together in the Temple every day.
They ate together in their homes,
happy to share their food with joyful hearts.

ACTS 2:46

Cooking with grandkids is easy during the holidays. They are often in the kitchen snatching samples!

Our modern food culture plays a central role in life today. Demands for healthier alternatives, economical choices, global options, and the "buy local" movement will all be reflected during holiday meals. Of course, when a heritage recipe is baking in the oven, the sweet smell is all that's needed to trigger memories of years passed.

Creating new memories doesn't require a miniature chef's hat (although it provides great photo ops). Mashing avocados for guacamole or decorating cookies with candy sprinkles are simple first steps to tackling lengthy family recipes when children are older.

Working together in the kitchen offers an ideal opportunity for casual conversation. During the holidays, children barely have time to warm up to a social setting before relatives ask, "What do you want for Christmas?" Most children are more open to talking when they are doing something and aren't put on the spot.

Making or baking something to give away allows your child to participate in what early Christians experienced as they shared "food with joyful hearts." Being affirmed for generosity isn't the reason you and your grandchild spend time preparing food gifts, but it offers a useful way to participate in holiday giving.

To Do with My Grandchild

Compile a book or box with favorite family recipes to give to a grandchild. Include more than ingredients and directions; add notes about the people who made the food, how and when it was served, and any other information that will help your grandchild visualize the time and place. Describe the smells and tastes that still connect emotionally with you. Every detail can be significant in telling the story of food that was meaningful in your personal family history.

To Pray

Dear God,

Thank you for the special opportunities to connect with my grandchild during the holidays. As we go about our activities, please help us prepare room in our hearts to welcome the birth of your Son. Amen.

To Reflect

During this holiday season, I want to help my grandchild...

_____

_____

_____

_____

_____

_____

_____

_____

_____

_____

_____

_____

_____

_____

_____

50

Peace

I give you peace, the kind of peace that only I can give.
It isn't like the peace that this world can give.
So don't be worried or afraid.

JOHN 14:27 CEV

Are you overwhelmed yet?

As the Christmas countdown descends, stress often bubbles up. Emotions run wild. Although children typically misbehave if they are tired or hungry, waiting impatiently for Grandma can trigger wild behavior too. The message of "peace on earth" can get buried under holiday-induced drama that erupts even in loving families.

Fear that everything on the to-do list won't get checked off makes it feel like life is spiraling out of bounds. Yet God's peace communicates that He is in control. His peace equips us to deflect the commercialism and non-Christ-centered messages that woo us away from Bethlehem.

Leaving faith footprints reflects God's gift of peace. You and your grandchild might move around the manger figures under the tree to retell the story of the first Christmas. Or, perhaps you and your grandchild hang baby shoes from each family member on the Christmas tree as a reminder that Jesus came to earth as a baby. During the days before Christmas, you might eat dinner by the light of battery-operated candles as a reminder that Jesus is the light of the world.

As you and grandchild shift away from holiday noise, your actions remind the entire family that we all thank God for the gift of His peace at Christmas.

To Do with My Grandchild

Instead of checking off a to-do list, ask your grandchild to help write a "don't do" list. Simply think of holiday activities and events that aren't related to the real meaning of Christmas; in our commercially driven universe, even young children can generate a lengthy list. Just reading a list of all the nice-but-not-necessary activities can reduce the stress. Even if you participate in some cherished customs on the "don't do" list, repeatedly return to reminders of the first Christmas through songs, books, and Christ-centered traditions.

To Pray

Dear God,
Fill the hearts of loved ones with the peace that only you can give. Send the Holy Spirit to strengthen the connections between us all during these busy days before Christmas. Amen.

To Reflect

I pray that I have helped my grandchild learn that Christmas...

_____

_____

_____

_____

_____

_____

_____

_____

_____

_____

_____

_____

_____

_____

_____

_____

_____

51

Smell Christmas

*God uses us to spread his knowledge everywhere
like a sweet-smelling perfume.*

2 CORINTHIANS 2:14

Breathe deeply.

Does pine mingle with gingerbread? Or do other holiday fragrances float through the air? Many memories of Christmas are tinged with scents that unfortunately include calories but always shout, "It's Christmas!"

God created our grandchildren with the ability to smell even before birth. Newborns depend on smell more than any other sense. Throughout life, our sense of smell is the first alert to danger; we smell a fire before we see flames, and we know there's a gas leak without seeing anything. This is a good time to pause and thank God for our nose.

During St. Paul's third missionary journey, he compares the smell of incense burned during a victory parade in Rome to the way that knowledge of Jesus Christ is spread among His people. This sweet perfume is transmitted wherever people come to know Jesus.

The holidays offer windows of opportunity to share the Good News with friends and relatives we rarely see. The carols we sing and traditions we participate in often reference the birth of Jesus. God can use us to become the "sweet smell of Christ." Like Aaron and other long-ago priests who were anointed with oil, God drenches us in sweet spiritual perfume to carry His message of salvation.

We light candles with holiday aromas and create sweet and savory foods in the kitchen, but "wearing the sweet smell of Christ among those who are being saved" is God's fragrant gift to us and those we meet.

To Do with My Grandchild

Many varieties of dried and fresh fruit are available during the holidays. You and your grandchild can set up a sniff test for your next meal. Line up holiday muffin cups or small bowls down the center of your table. Your grandchild will love to drop samples of a single type of fruit in each cup: oranges, dates, papaya, apple slices, pineapple, mango, banana chips, cranberries, etc. (Large pieces can be a choking hazard, so dice the fruit for young children.) Lay a piece of paper on top of each cup. Your grandchild will delight in watching family members smell the fruit before revealing what's in each cup. In the mealtime prayer, thank God for the many holiday foods that taste and smell so good.

To Pray

Dear God,
The sights, sounds, and scents of the holidays are among the many blessings for which I give thanks today. Sharing these with my grandchild will give me more memories to treasure. Thank you. Amen.

To Reflect

A fragrant memory my grandchild and I both associate with Christmas is...

_____

_____

_____

_____

_____

_____

_____

_____

_____

_____

_____

_____

_____

_____

_____

52

Holy Ground

"Do not come any closer," God said. "Take off your sandals, for the place where you are standing is holy ground."

EXODUS 3:5 NIV

Reflection comes naturally as things end. We think back to the end of each day, the last day of vacation, or the final day on the calendar. We have closure before each new beginning.

What do you remember about the past year? The satisfaction of carrying on a tradition? The love conveyed a tight hug?

Some moments seem to have a deeper dimension. At those times, we sense that a conversation or a situation has more than ordinary significance. Some call those "holy moments" or "God sightings"—times when we are more aware of the presence of God. In these instances, we're reminded that God is always with us.

Moses had a holy moment at the burning bush. In the presence of God, Moses was commanded to take off his sandals because he was standing on holy ground. And yet, wherever God walks He works, and that is holy ground.

The space between you and a grandchild at the kitchen table is holy ground. The space between you and a daughter-in-law is holy ground. The space between you and the "other" grandmother is holy ground, because wherever God walks, He works. That place becomes holy ground.

As you close this book, stay alert for times when God makes His presence known, for at that moment, you might be standing on holy ground.

To Do with My Grandchild

We are aware of the big things of life in which God is active, but draw your grandchild's attention to the little things we often take for granted. A young child typically comes to know God as the Creator, so a toddler or preschooler will look for signs of God in a snowflake, sunset, or new puppy. Older grandchildren become more aware of the ways that God works through people or in situations. But people of all ages have an identical takeaway: When you look for God at work, you see how busy He is.

To Pray

Dear God,
I am so grateful for the many times you have shown me signs of your presence, your peace, and your power. Today and always, help me see your hand in my life, knowing that all good comes from you. Amen.

To Reflect

The times when I feel God's presence...

_____

_____

_____

_____

_____

_____

_____

_____

_____

_____

_____

_____

_____

_____

_____

_____

_____

_____